FOUR

# Fourteen

GAIL McCONNELL

Green Bottle Press

First published in 2018
by Green Bottle Press
83 Grove Avenue
London N10 2AL
www.greenbottlepress.com

All rights reserved

© Gail McConnell, 2018

The right of Gail McConnell to be identified
as author of this work has been asserted in accordance
with the Copyright, Designs and Patents Act, 1988

Cover design by Økvik Design
Typeset by CB editions, London
Printed in England by Imprint Digital, Exeter EX5 5HY

ISBN 978 1 910804 11 7

**LOTTERY FUNDED**

# Contents

| | |
|---|---|
| Cycle Route 9 | 1 |
| Twenty Three Fifteen | 2 |
| Worm | 8 |
| Headline | 9 |
| Narwhal | 10 |
| Octopus | 11 |
| Mobile | 12 |
| 0 | 16 |
| Ampersand | 19 |
| Start Out | 20 |
| Narwhal | 22 |
| Octopus | 23 |
| Imprint, O Lord, thy word | 24 |
| Figure | 25 |
| 14 | 26 |

# Cycle Route 9

Our love it lives at 6.3 degrees.
I stooped to measure it inside a dream.
A meagre distance. Not the moon in apogee.
Still, from earth it rises at a tilt unseen.
The sun a decade older than before
first words (on the second-hand-furniture
warehouse concrete floor in BT4),
our love some saw – still see – as forfeiture.

Love – it is not love until it's tested.
So wrote Kierkegaard. Or sang that icon,
Lady Gaga. Hills already crested,
no sudden stops – our tyres revolving on
the long canal towpath through Portadown
& up to where we are, so startlingly set down.

## Twenty Three Fifteen

Don't look at the sun.

*

This is the last thing
that you tell me
before you leave.
Or one of the last things.

*

You could look at it
through a colander.
That's another.

*

The thought of standing in the garden
with a colander on my head
is not appealing.
Then I watch a video online.
Stupid pre-caffeinated me.

*

I read that the birds will stop singing.

*

The first time I kissed you
we were in the dark.
I walked you home
as the sun came up
over Connswater.

*

We had been a secret
from everyone
including, at first,
ourselves.

*

These last few weeks have been

*

I am going downstairs to find the colander.

*

The grout between the tiles
on the bathroom floor
began to crack and shift
as this began to happen.
I think about the ground
beneath our feet. The grout
sticks to our soles.

*

I am not sure what just happened.

*

Black is white and cold is heat.

*

These celestial bodies
overlapping
in full view.

*

The sensation of a sharp-edged
sliver of grout
embedding in a slightly clammy
sole
that pads the tiles
this way and that way.

\*

Oh, my appetite for spectacle
and for other people's appetite
for spectacle and for other people's
tweets about their appetite for spectacle.

\*

Like a big dandelion head
made up of wee crescent curves
that piece of paper
I held up in the breeze.
I couldn't photograph the shape –
the flowery shadow with its punctures –
cos I had the colander in one hand
and the paper in the other.

\*

Trending and trending in the widening

\*

The night it all came out
I had my first panic attack.
Then my second
and my third.

\*

Bonnie Tyler's hair
is almost as big as ever.

*

Where am I
without some digital witness?

*

This thing we do
this life we share
terrifies me –
the truth our love
withstands.
Nothing
should be
this real,
surely,
these flimsy days?

*

I know you told me not to but I looked.

*

Self-portrait with red plastic
Swedish-made
colander under my arm.

*

There's this thing
you do with your mouth
when you zip up your jeans
the same shape

every day
sort of an awww
sounding shape
as if you are going to say
orange
or oracle
or ordinary
or orbicular
or orchestrate
or organism
or original sin
or orientate
or orbital.

*

Let's do this together
in 2026.

*

My eyes feel wonky or maybe I'm imagining it.

*

I didn't see them at first,
those sickle-shaped nothings
surrounded by shadow.
The colander was too close
to the paper. When I pulled it back
I said *wow* then heard my neighbour's
smartphone click a photo
and felt stupid for a moment
and then thought she is stupid
for taking a shit photo of the sun

and then wanted to share with her
this evidence and then thought
I'm probably holding it wrong
and those curves are just the curves
of the holes in IKEA's design.

\*

Cloud and moon and sun –
one obscures another.

\*

There's a looping time-lapse video online:
the sun contracting then expanding
in negative space.

\*

I love that you
unzipped
your mouth
unconscious awww
every sleepy morning.

\*

Turn around bright eyes
don't leave.

## Worm

Burrowing in your allotted patch you
    move through the dark, muscles contracting one by one

in every part, lengthening and shortening
    the slick segmented tube of you, furrows in your wake.

Devising passages for water, air,
    you plot the gaps that keep the structure from collapse.

Dead things you know. Plants and creatures both.
    Your grooves shift matter, sifting as you go.

Eyeless, your appetite aerates.
    Eating the world, you open it.

You ingest to differentiate.
    Under the foot-stamped earth, you eat into a clot

of leaf mould, clay and mildew, and express what you can
    part with, as self-possessed as when you started.

Your secretions bind the soil,
    your shit enriches it. How things lie

now will be undone, will reoccur. You, a surface-level archivist
    sensing all there is

can be gone through. The body borne
    within its plot.

## Headline

Holes in the sand are
more dangerous than sharks.
The lark of it is this: our own
stupid hand gives death

a kick-start – not the fin
in the water but the moat
that we build before
falling right in.

# Narwhal

This living under glass is all he knows.
Or living with its threat –
the encroachment
of ice. In Arctic waters
the corpse whale roams.

The fear of suffocation
drives echolocation.

The echo after pulse
confirms / denies
the dot dot dash dot wish
to live with news of air holes
or their lack.

That horn which is not horn
but tooth, biologists misread.

Jousting lance, they said, his tusk
which seemed less tusk than sword –
a nine-foot spiral-structured blade.

Perforated to perfection, it's a survival aid.
Our bare life prompts invention.

## Octopus

With no internal shell you keep
yourself together in a sac
& the matter of attachment.

All you know you know by touch; shape,
texture and scale you draw into
the mouth of every flowering cup.

From pit to tip the suckers spring.
Each flicker of skin criss-crossing
your path a chance to make contact,

a chance to draw a body not
your own into your care, or spread
out into theirs. The emptiness

you know you've laboured to transpose.
Your vacuum sets their course, carries
these objects of desire towards

your hearts so that they hold; hemmed in
in eight soft limbs and the borders
of concavities, folded fast.

The things that cling can't always be
predicted – slivers of mirror,
bits of bone, curls, keys, a toy gun.

Attachment: is it grace or grasp?
All things unknown familiar in
the peeling off & letting go.

# Mobile

### 0

I text
you text me
back we go
round & round
like this
tap it
out read
it through our
hours
over

### 1

it's lost – the code – no use – no sound
_ _ _ _ – demand – unanswered

### 2

ting ting
the sound
it makes

my head
ting ting
pick up

press me
open
ting ting

you type
the text
thumb thumb

ting ting
touch here
enter

passcode
try try
again

ting ting
slide to
unlock

    3

it's dead
again I press

    on

the key again
nothing

    4

it goes off in
the small hours

a voice you
can't make

out saying please
don't please stop

5

          Mail     an envelope
    Open hand     privacy

  Conjoined men     find friends
    Your health     a cornered heart

  Do not disturb     the moon

6

you call
this
your cell

a single
store
a room
and door

a chamber
locked
loaded

7

I follow you
don't follow
me

delete
the list
and you

can't see

**8**

    Touch the icon    Magnify

**9**

it rings
out

the sound

out from
the chamber

the news
not out

yet

# 0

The last day
   we went up there
we saw something

a sperm comet
   sitting in the hallway

       o

darkness was over
   the surface of the deep

       o

that was the day
   of the snow moon
and the lunar eclipse

       o

every one is sacred
every one is great

       o

we didn't take
   the time to look

our bodies stayed
   our thoughts
on this

       o

What the hell is a sperm comet?
*The SpermComet® test is a Male Infertility Test*
*that measures damaged DNA*
*in individual sperm.*

    o

that was also the day
   the New Year comet
would approach

    o

THERE'S a single sperm with its DNA damage blazing in
   its wake

    o

   o not o:::::::
is what they want
   to see

    o

one on the floor and one in the sky

    o

What is a good omen? *People also ask*
Can a pregnant woman go to a funeral?
What snakes represent in dreams?
What does it mean when you see a dead bird?

    o

They call the day
   they take the eggs

from you & introduce
   them to the sperm
Day Zero

     o

O long-haired star, burn on for us.

## Ampersand

A rope trick
A mangled anchor
A misshapen treble clef
A knot instruction illustration
A figure eight with benefits
A bind
An Et in Trebuchet like a backwards B
A lemniscate gone rogue
An infinity upended and enlarged

                    by ligature

& more & more & more & more &

## Start Out

It's not the thought of being hoicked out
with tongs that bothers me. It's the fact you're out
and out unsure. The facts you can't or won't spell out.
'The age I was, I think they must've knocked me out
and hauled you out with forceps.' It comes out
over tea and scones, an out-of-date
currant pinched in thumb and forefinger as out
the story comes quite out
of the blue. 'I was out
of action for a while, of course, but better to be out
of danger than in them stirrups, your legs outflung
and all akimbo. You'd have to be out
of your mind. At 40 I wanted out
of harm's way. So I didn't push you out.
The cons, as they say, outweighed
the pros. Or was it the other way? Them lifting you out,
is that the risky bit? I can't figure it out.
Not at my age. The days, they merge. Out
goes the light and you wake up to another. Soon I'll be out
of this world for good. Over and out.'

Like a Foxrock wife or mouth straight out
of Beckett, via Belfast, this imagined mother reads out
her lines before I catch myself at it and the thing gets out
of hand, the monologue outsourced
from here or there, like the one with all the hands, singled out
for praise by those in the know. So. Out
with it, I suppose. It's the Long Kesh breakout
I've been thinking of, and all that came before. And after.
                                                    Time out

of mind. The faces looking back at you when you look out
the peephole. The blankets handed out.
The breakfasts measured out.
The returned counted out.
The spray gun painting 'Brits Out'.
The spray gun painting 'Taigs Out'.
The insides painted out.
POs and SOs out
of their depth, so out
on sick leave. In or out
of the cell, all under one roof & all hung out
to dry as the reruns loop out
over the airwaves – crime is crime is crime – until it cuts out.
The brick, it hits the radio full whack. Knockout.

Did you think about getting out?
I don't know why you stuck it out
or started it at all. And when those men came out
of the house across the way, guns out,
and up the drive, what words fell out
of your mouth before you couldn't get them out?

I never quite came – Out!
The umpire calls it. Outside
the line. The Wimbledon camera zooms out.
The connection has timed out.

Theseus spins it out,
the yarn he tells about that clew and catching out
the beast, howling out
in pain, as though he'd first sketched it out.
Ariadne knows the thing that holds it all can't quite be
                                                                               straightened out.

# Narwhal

The beast receives and reads the sea
that purls into each cavity.
He knows where icebergs melt
and form
by measuring salinity.

Any loss of sensitivity
is deathly here, he knows,
though the ocean spreads below,
the ice above, on on it goes – the capture
and release of water in the hollows.

The problem is the cure –
the scouring and discharging sea.

Salt accrues in apertures –
the price of intimacy.

## Octopus

Panicked, with inky melanin
you make a slipstream to get free
or make autotomy an art

rewriting your anatomy.
Camouflage has failed, mimicry
cannot hold off attack. Scoring

your arms with incisions those claws.
Whose cuts are these? Who bruises, chews
at your skin, initiates this

severing? You watch it detach,
float away from you. Coppered blood
infuses the already blue.

Self-sabotage, the first and last
stage of collage, the cutting up
without the glue. The bitten limb

goes unattached, but is renewed.
You didn't know you knew the art
of self-repair until alone

those hundred days, watching something
grow. New cups bloom the length of you;
mouths opening by small degrees.

The whipping fins can be withstood,
the gripping jaws. All that issues
from the deep, in all likelihood.

# Imprint, O Lord, thy word

A Father holds the thumb of his right hand
to his neighbour's forehead
                        the oil within its whorl
                                transferred without a word.

This press is an anointing, the last
the man will know before his body
is interred.
            The blood drains from the hole
made newly in his back       as the man with special powers
                        initiates the round-up.

The Father stands up from the body.
His molecules vibrate at the point from where
the bullet enters
                        the message passed
                from cell to cell as the circulation
        slows.

He touches to his face
his thumb

    the spirals turning inward

        oil and smoke, a siren somewhere, eyelids start
            to close

    lips meet
        and part

            in the – O – O – O –

of prayer

# Figure

Walking at the water's edge, a curlew.
Stilt legs hinge one two one two one two.

Step-stepping on the mud, the lough in view;
and out of sight, the worms. Casts are the clue.

It spears the ground, maintaining its hairdo,
& sucks what isn't there & swallows too.

Its slender bill is perfect for fondue,
a pair of tongs whose curve is not a curlicue.

Underground worms wriggle in the snafu.
And so it goes, each meal impromptu.

Dead poets formed the bird in solemn hue
in mourning for some loss, forever blue.

The keening in its cry is not untrue.
Adieu – again – my thoughts turn back to you.

## 14

Like trying to get a speck of sand from inside a jelly,
is what one of the forums said. I picture you shaking
a big red jelly sculpted in a curvy silver mould
sitting on a bone-white oval enamel plate.

Again and again – and now, again – I picture it.
The sand does not come loose.

\*

A friend tells us a friend
is moving to a valley in the Peak District. I raise my glass
to Hope, she raises hers, you lift your water glass.

\*

To remove or turn out of a place of lodgement; to displace.
To shift the position of (a force).
To drive (a foe) out of his position.
To drive (a beast) out of its lair.
To go away from one's lodging or abode; to quit the place
    where one is lodged; to remove.
To leave a place of encampment.
To leave a resting-place.

\*

On the fifth day you worry that by lightly jogging across
    the road for the bus you've done some damage.

You revise the light jog as a quick shuffle.

We ponder whether this is better or worse.

\*

Our friends who are mothers say *be positive. Light a candle.
   Take this penny. Picture it.*
Their daughter takes steamed asparagus in her fists and
   gums it.

   *

We play with Kensey, Ben and Joseph. I am afraid
   they will run out of the playpark and away
but all they want to do is to be chased.

   *

My family comes for Mother's Day. Lamb tagine
   and chocolate torte and then a walk to walk it off.

We stop to hear the pine cones cracking in the heat,
   each one slowly opening.

   *

And the evening and the morning were the eleventh day.

   *

On the thirteenth we spend the afternoon in bed. It's blank there in my iCal. I rush to join a seminar on the autonomist Marxists and precarious labour. *The refusal of work does not negate one nexus of capitalist society, one aspect of capital's process of production or reproduction.* Ten minutes in you text.

Blood. Later, not.

   *

I watch a Berger documentary. Tilda peeling apples
   the way his father did it. Think of ways of seeing, what
   he said about the naked / nude antimony.
   Antimony?

That's what I've noted down but do I mean one of the
   elementary bodies, a brittle metallic substance, of
   bright bluish white colour and flaky crystalline texture?

An alloy, paired with lead, for making batteries, bullets,
   organ pipes? Used to stop the flames that try to eat
   at fire-proof things?

Tilda adapts her style. Another popular etymology
   is the hypothetical Greek word ἀντίμόνος *antimonos*,
   'against aloneness'.

\*

Everyone knows sucking a pineapple core won't work
   but isn't it tempting?
So what of abstention in the two-week wait?

\*

Pour down upon us the abundance of your mercy,
   forgiving us those things of which
our conscience is afraid.

\*

Your mother sends us a day-by-day she downloaded.
The bubbles multiply.

## Acknowledgements

Thanks to the editors of the following journals in which some of these poems were first published: 'Twenty Three Fifteen' in *The Manchester Review*; 'Worm' and 'Start Out' in *PN Review*; 'Narwhal' in *past simple*; '14' in *The Tangerine*. The last three words of 'Cycle Route 9' are taken from Annie Dillard, *Pilgrim at Tinker Creek* (New York: HarperPerennial, 1998). My thanks to everyone at the Tyrone Guthrie Centre at Annaghmakerrig. I am grateful to the Arts Council of Northern Ireland for a bursary to support the development of this pamphlet.

Thank you to those who have read and encouraged the work, in particular: Vahni Capildeo, Colin Graham, Richard Holloway, Mimi Khalvati, Alice Lyons, Damian Smyth, George Szirtes and Tess Taylor. Thanks to the Old Daffs; and to students and colleagues at Queen's University Belfast. Thank you, Ciaran Carson – reader at my elbow with cortados on the table down on Lombard Street; I love our conversations. Thank you, Jean, for giving me a line. I am grateful to my editor, Jennifer Grigg, for reading the work with care and seeing the poems into print. To my parents and my family on both sides of the Atlantic, my thanks and love.

Above all, my love –

Beth, thank you &c.

And then there's the one who came along after I thought the acknowledgements were complete, and who has changed everything forever. Thank you, Finn.